W9-APS-260

Skeletons and Exoskeletons

by Julie K. Lundgren

Science Content Editor:
Shirley Duke

Educational Media

rourkeeducationalmedia.com

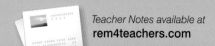

Teacher Notes available at
rem4teachers.com

Science Content Editor: Shirley Duke holds a bachelor's degree in biology and a master's degree in education from Austin College in Sherman, Texas. She taught science in Texas at all levels for twenty-five years before starting to write for children. Her science books include *You Can't Wear These Genes, Infections, Infestations, and Diseases, Enterprise STEM, Forces and Motion at Work, Environmental Disasters,* and *Gases.* She continues writing science books and also works as a science content editor.

www.rourkeeducationalmedia.com

Photo credits: Cover © happy SUN, Ivancovlad, Cosmin Manci; Table of Contents © Arcady; Page 4 © Leah-Anne Thompson; Page 4/5 © A. Petelin; Page 6 © liubomir; Page 7 © Vittorio Bruno; Page 6/7 © Arcady; Page 8 © Pling; Page 8/9 © alslutsky; Page 10 © Fotocrisis; Page 11 © James Steidl; Page 10/11 © Ami Beyer; Page 12 © vblinov; Page 13 © Dorling Kindersley; Page 12/13 © Mark Skalny; Page 14 © Sebastian Kaulitzki, Reha Mark; Page 15 © alxhar, Stacy Barnett; Page 16 © Gelpi, srdjan draskovic, William Attard McCarthy, Page 17 © CLIPAREA | Custom media, gracious_tiger; Page 18/19 © pandapaw; Page 19 © liubomir, Sklmsta; Page 20 © Hugh Lansdown, Victor Tyakht; Page 21 © Yuri Arcurs;

Editor: Kelli Hicks

My Science Library series produced by Nicola Stratford Design, Florida for Rourke Educational Media.

Library of Congress PCN Data

Lundgren, Julie K.
 Skeletons and Exoskeletons / Julie K. Lundgren.
    p. cm. -- (My Science Library)
 ISBN 978-1-61810-088-7 (Hard cover) (alk. paper)
 ISBN 978-1-61810-221-8 (Soft cover)
 Library of Congress Control Number: 2012930291

Rourke Educational Media
Printed in the United States of America,
North Mankato, Minnesota

rourkeeducationalmedia.com

customerservice@rourkeeducationalmedia.com • PO Box 643328 Vero Beach, Florida 32964

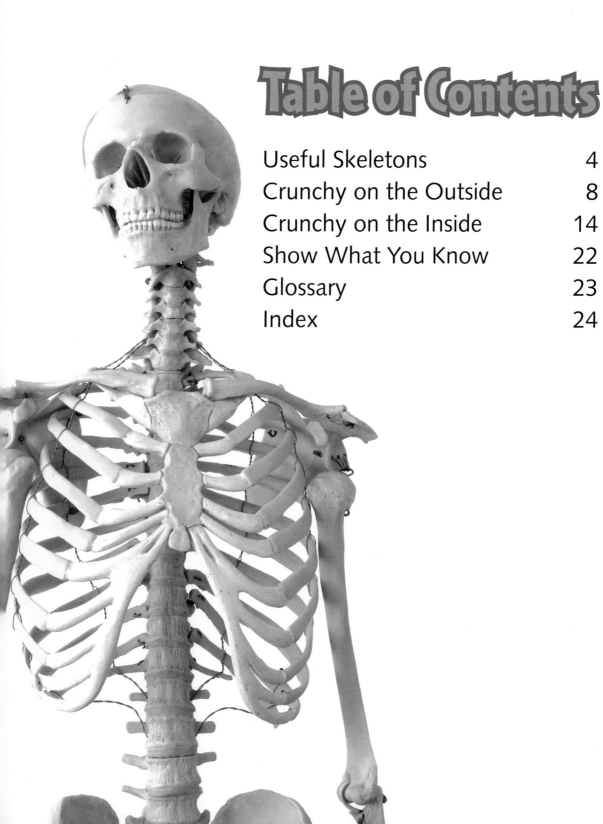

Table of Contents

Useful Skeletons

Animals and people have skeletons to protect and support the inner workings of their bodies. **Muscles** attach to skeletons so we can move.

Skeletal muscles allow us to skip, jump, sprint, and swim.

Skeletons give bodies shape, strength, and the ability to bend and twist.

Animals with exoskeletons have skeletons on the outside of their bodies. You can see exoskeletons. Turtles, ants, grasshoppers, and other insects have exoskeletons.

Animals with skeletons inside their bodies have endoskeletons. Bony fish like the ocean sunfish and the Atlantic blue marlin have endoskeletons.

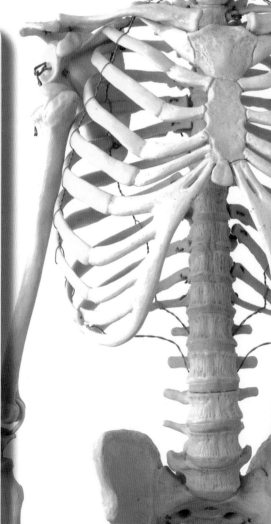

People have endoskeletons.

A Bone To Pick

Turtles have an endoskeleton, parts of which have adapted into what looks like a bony case. A turtle's upper and lower shells function as an exoskeleton.

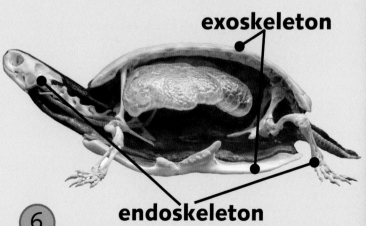

exoskeleton

endoskeleton

No Skeleton? No Problem!

Animals with soft bodies do not have any skeleton at all. These animals include octopus, jellyfish, and earthworms. The water or soil they live in provides their support. They protect themselves in other ways.

Although an octopus is without a skeleton, water supports its body. It protects itself by blending into its surroundings and squirting ink to help it escape predators.

Crunchy on the Outside

Animals with exoskeletons do not have bones. Exoskeletons often have **segments**. Exoskeletons may be thinner near joints. Segments and joints help skeletons bend and move easily. Minerals, **chitin**, and **proteins** make exoskeletons hard and crunchy.

The New Candy?

Chitin is a strong material made of sugars bonded together. Does this make an insect taste sweet? No, but people say raw or roasted insects can taste like bacon, popcorn, nuts, lemons, or seafood.

green June beetle

Most of Earth's animals have exoskeletons.

Animals with exoskeletons live on land and in water. Insects, spiders, shrimp, crabs, and lobsters all have exoskeletons. Some **mollusks**, like clams, do too. Scientists estimate that over 3 million different kinds of animals with exoskeletons live on Earth.

African giant millipedes' many segments allow them to curl up or turn easily.

Exoskeletons do not grow. Instead, the animal **molts** and grows a new, larger exoskeleton. Animals with exoskeletons, especially land animals, cannot grow very big. The thickness and weight of a large animal's exoskeleton would limit movement.

A dragonfly changes from wingless nymph to adult through molting.

Just after molting, the new exoskeleton is soft for a time. Until it dries and hardens, the animal is helpless. Predators find freshly molted animals easy to eat. Gulls, shorebirds, and sea stars enjoy eating freshly molted crabs.

Maine lobster

One of the largest animals with an exoskeleton is the Maine lobster. Compare this to the largest animal with an endoskeleton, the blue whale. A blue whale can span a basketball court.

blue whale

Crunchy on the Inside

Animals with endoskeletons have bones. Special bones protect organs like the heart, lungs, and brain. The minerals in bones make them hard, but bones also contain tough **fibers** to make them strong.

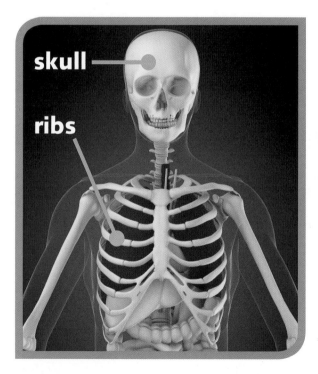

skull

ribs

A skull protects the brain. Ribs form a cage around the heart and lungs.

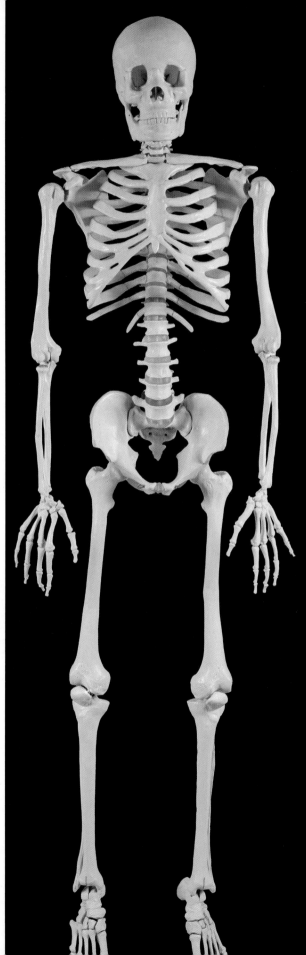

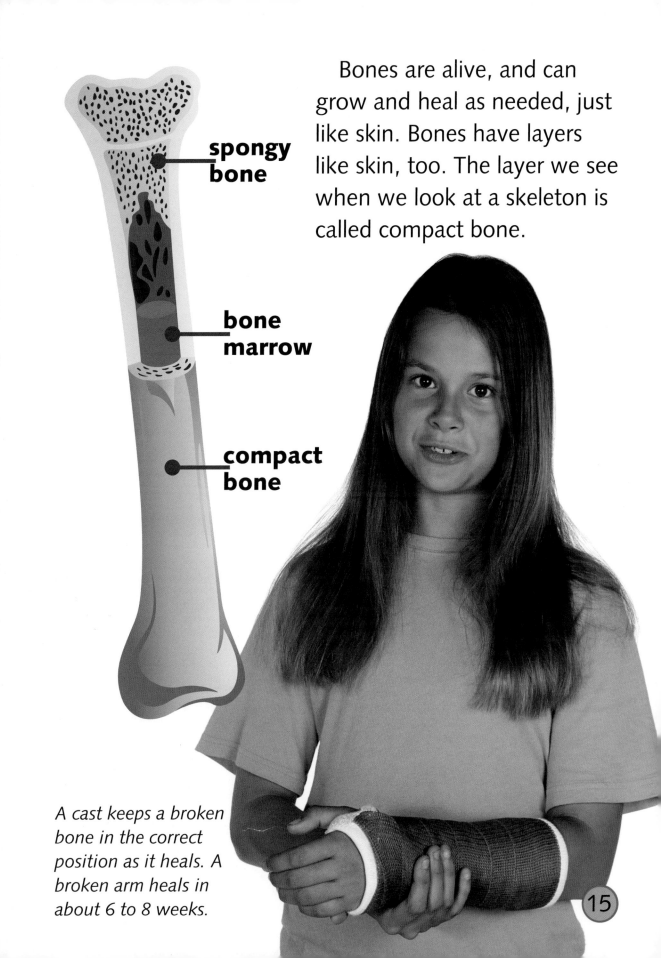

spongy bone

bone marrow

compact bone

Bones are alive, and can grow and heal as needed, just like skin. Bones have layers like skin, too. The layer we see when we look at a skeleton is called compact bone.

A cast keeps a broken bone in the correct position as it heals. A broken arm heals in about 6 to 8 weeks.

Animal groups with endoskeletons include birds, reptiles, bony fish, **amphibians**, and **mammals**. Mammals are animals with fur or hair, and include people.

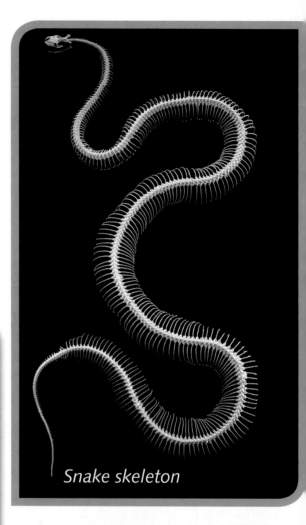

Snake skeleton

A Bone To Pick

A funny bone is not a bone at all. When you bump your elbow, you hit a nerve that runs close to the surface of your skin.

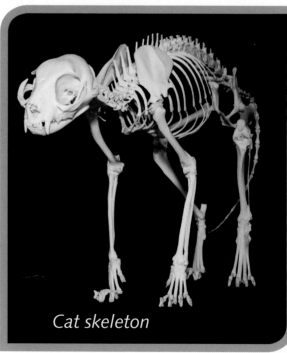

Cat skeleton

The number of bones in endoskeletons varies with age and from one kind of animal to another. A human baby may have over 270 bones. Over time certain bones **fuse** together, like skull bones, so an adult has about 206 bones. All mammals, however, have seven neck bones, even giraffes!

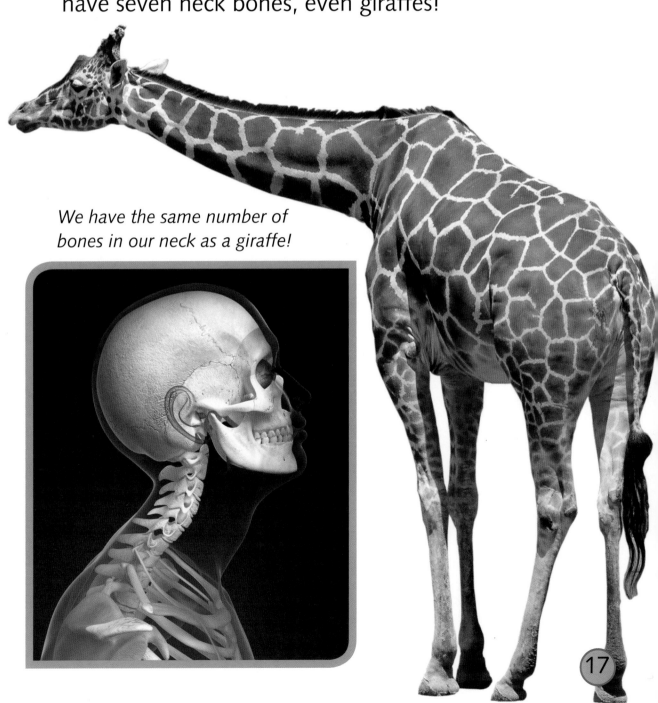

We have the same number of bones in our neck as a giraffe!

Animals have bone **adaptations** to help them fit their environment. Heavy animals like elephants have large, thick bones for support.

Many birds have bones with thin layers of compact bone and hollow cores for easier flight. A lightweight bird does not need as much energy to lift itself into the air.

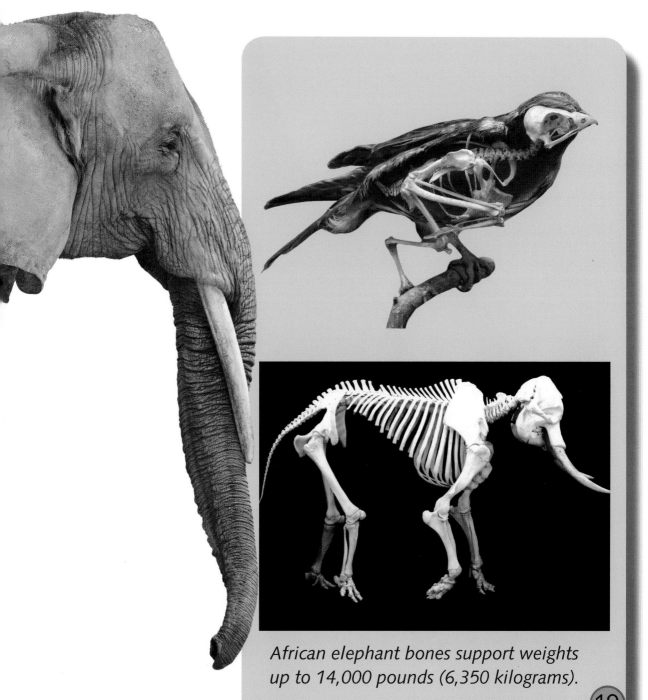

African elephant bones support weights up to 14,000 pounds (6,350 kilograms).

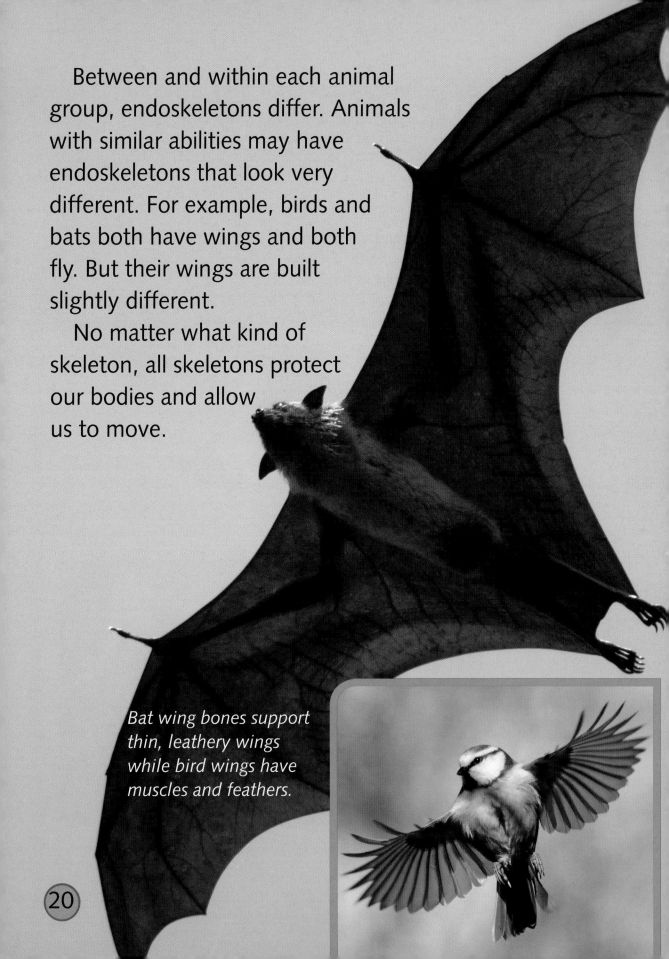

Between and within each animal group, endoskeletons differ. Animals with similar abilities may have endoskeletons that look very different. For example, birds and bats both have wings and both fly. But their wings are built slightly different.

No matter what kind of skeleton, all skeletons protect our bodies and allow us to move.

Bat wing bones support thin, leathery wings while bird wings have muscles and feathers.

Explore Your World!

Choose a habitat to explore, like a playground, backyard, pond, or beach. You'll need:

- Pencil and paper
- Clipboard
- Collection cups
  (clean, white butter containers work well)
- A magnifying glass
- A small, fine net
- Binoculars

Use the cups, net, magnifying glass and binoculars as tools to find animals. Dip a cup into the weedy water of a pond and inspect your water sample. Do you see anything moving? Use the magnifying glass to find tiny swimmers. Swish the net over the tops of grasses or flowers to capture crawling or flying insects. Use the binoculars to get a close up look at birds or other animals in trees or shrubs. List or draw the animals you find. What kinds of skeletons do they have? Are there more animals with exoskeletons or endoskeletons?

After studying captured animals, gently release them back into their habitat.

Show What You Know

1. Name three animals with exoskeletons.

2. Why do Earth's largest animals have endoskeletons?

3. How do animals with no skeletons protect themselves?

Glossary

adaptations (ad-ap-TAY-shunz): changes in animals over time that help them live

amphibians (am-FIB-ee-ins): animals that live part of their lives in water and part out of water, like frogs and toads

chitin (KYE-tin): a strong, natural material often found in exoskeletons

fibers (FYE-burz): threads of tough, flexible material found in plants and animals

fuse (FEWZ): to join together two objects, like bones, to form one object that cannot be separated

mammals (MAM-uhlz): a group of animals, including people, that have hair or fur and make milk for their young

mollusks (MOL-uhsks): water animals without bones, some of whom can make a protective shell, like clams

molts (MOHLTZ): to shed the outer layer in order to grow

muscles (MUHSS-uhlz): the parts of the body that perform the work of moving

proteins (PROH-teenz): materials the body makes and uses for strength and health

segments (SEG-muhnts): divided parts that make up the body or exoskeleton

Index

Websites to Visit

http://kidshealth.org/kid/htbw/bones.html

http://yucky.discovery.com/flash/body/pg000124.html

www.oum.ox.ac.uk/thezone/animals/life/move.htm

About the Author

Julie K. Lundgren has written more than 40 nonfiction books for children. She gets a kick out of sharing juicy facts about science, nature, and animals, especially if they are slightly disgusting! Through her work, she hopes kids will learn that Earth is an amazing place and young people can make a big difference in keeping our planet healthy. She lives in Minnesota with her family.

Ask The Author!
www.rem4students.com